RETURNINGS

RETURNINGS

• • • • •

Life-after-Death Experiences:
A Christian View

JOHN R. AURELIO

CONTINUUM · NEW YORK

1995

The Continuum Publishing Company
370 Lexington Avenue, New York, NY 10017

Printed in the United States of America

Library of Congress Cataloging-in-Publication Data

Aurelio, John.
  Returnings : life-after-death experiences : a Christian view /
John R. Aurelio.
     p.   cm.
  Includes bibliographical references.
  ISBN 0-8264-0789-7 (alk. paper)
  1. Resurrection.   2. Future life—Christianity.   3. Jesus Christ—
Resurrection.   I. Title.
BT872.A87   1995
236′.8—dc20   94-42564
                                                         CIP

CONTENTS

Contents

PREFACE

C hristian tradition holds that for fifty days after the resurrection, Jesus repeatedly reappeared to any number of people.

> But God raised him from the dead and for many days he appeared to those who came up with him from Galilee to Jerusalem, and they are now his witnesses to the people.
> *Acts 13:30–31*[1]

For I handed on to you as of first importance what I in turn had received: that Christ died for our sins in accordance with the Scriptures, and that he was buried, and that he was raised on the third day in accordance with the Scriptures, and that he appeared to Cephas, then to the twelve. Then he appeared to more than five hundred brothers and sisters at one time, most of whom are still alive, though some have died. Then he appeared to James, then to all the apostles. Last of all, as to one untimely born, he appeared also to me.

1 Corinthians 15:3–8

Once Jesus resurrected from the dead why did he not remain among the people and live with them as before? What was it that occasioned his reappearances? Why was it that only those who believed saw him?

These are unavoidable questions for every thinking person let alone every Christian. Furthermore, it seems to me that if we knew what it was that caused Jesus' reappearances we might use the same circumstances to bring him back again and again in our time? After all didn't he make the claim:

Know that I am with you always, until the end of the world.

Matthew 28:20

Jesus also claimed that whatever he did his followers would do and more.

Very truly, I tell you, the one who believes in me will also do the works that I do and, in fact, will do greater works than these, because I am going to the Father.

John 14:12

Resurrection in the Christian context doesn't mean that Jesus simply rose from the dead to return to the

Father never to be heard from again. Jesus is still living and acting in the world today. If such can be said of Jesus, the same must be said of all those who died "in Christ."

> The saying is sure: If we have died with him,
> we will also live with him.
>
> *2 Timothy 2:11*

If Jesus comes back, so must they. If we know how to bring Jesus back then we must also know how to make others return from the dead. How can it be otherwise?

NOTES

1. All Scripture quotations are from the New Revised Standard Version.

DEATH

There is nothing that is more
touching upon all of life
than the inevitability of death.

·1·

A QUESTION OF MORTALITY

Then Yahweh God gave . . . this admonition, "You may eat of all the trees in the garden. Nevertheless of the tree of the knowledge of good and evil you are not to eat, for on the day you eat of it you shall most surely die.

Genesis 2:16, 17

*D*eath! The End! Finis! The words have such a finality to them. "How can this be?" we ask ourselves. "How can death be the end?" We have asked this question in one form or another since the dawn of reason.

Is it all over when we die? Can the great door slam shut on who we are and what we are so that we are forever lost in oblivion? For those who believe in God the question is especially painful. "How can an all good and loving God allow us to die?"

What we are dealing with is the question of mortality. Do all living things die? As far as we know and can tell the answer is yes. Perhaps the question should be refined to mean only organic living things or life as we know it in the physical world since God is living and God will not die. The point is that all living things in our world are mortal. Life in the spiritual world is a mystery and a matter of faith.

The earth has faced death from the first moment that it faced life. Living things are by definition mortal. Life as we know it is terminal. It all comes to an end. Microscopic organisms die and giant sequoias die. Frail flowers and strong beasts die.[1]

How could it be otherwise? How could life on this planet continue without making way for new life? If life were not terminal, in no time at all earth would have been in one very sorry state of affairs. All the original life forms would have continued to exist so that before long there would have been a very serious problem of overpopulation. Of course, such life did not have to be procreative, which would have eliminated overcrowding. But, that would also have eliminated us since we were not among the original life forms. Either way we lose.

The question might also be, "How can an all good and loving God *not* allow for death?" Is the problem really death or our perception of it? Is that what the statement in Genesis, "For on the day you eat of it *you shall most surely* die," is alluding to? Not simply that we will die, which is inevitable but that death can be an abhorrent and frightful thing; that we will lose sight of the positive in it and see only the negative; that we can no longer see it as a good but only as an evil; that we have lost sight of the doughnut and can focus only on the hole.[2]

Death has been around since the inception of life. All we've been able to do over these many thousands of years is simply forestall it. But, we cannot avoid it or eliminate it.

> The days of our life are seventy years, or perhaps eighty, if we are strong; even then their span is only toil and trouble; they are soon gone, and we fly away.
>
> *Psalms 90:10*

Do we really have to? Do we really want to? Practically speaking, these are issues better faced when we are not confronted with our own imminent death when it would be difficult to be objective. However, if we prepare for it beforehand, we might be better able to deal with it when it does come.

Consider the endless ethical issues involved in overcrowding—who may procreate and may not; who will eventually have to make way for others; how will this "making way" happen? What about the aging process or do we assume that with the elimination of death perpetual youth would automatically follow? One might justifiably shudder imagining the problems physical immortality would occasion considering how poorly we've dealt with such scientific accomplishments as *in vitro* fertilization, genetic engineering, and the like. Would all necessary advancements have to follow along with immortality such as the end of all diseases, accidents, and misfortunes? Or worse still, what if they don't? What kind of brave, new world would that be?[3]

The problem is not so much death as our perception of it. Is Genesis trying to state that there would have been no death without sin or that sin would forever distort our view of it? Not simply that we would die—like the plants on the land, or the fish in the sea, or the birds of the air—but that we would *most surely die*, if we sinned. Given the assurance of our faith that there is a hereafter and that by our life choices we can go either to heaven or to hell, doesn't the possibility of eternal damnation imply that with death the damned would most surely have died?

> And in those days people will seek death but will not find it; they will long to die, but death will flee them.
>
> *Revelation 9:6*

Life is good and death is also good. It is sin that puts the sting in them both.

The sting of death is sin.

1 Corinthians 15:56

Death is the door from the physical world to the spiritual world,

> But someone has testified somewhere, "What are human beings that you are mindful of them, or mortals, that you care for them? You have made them *for a little while* lower than the angels; you have crowned them with glory and honor.
>
> *(Italics mine) Hebrews 2:6, 7*

from the imperfect to the perfect,

> He will wipe every tear from their eyes. Death will be no more; mourning and crying and pain will be no more, for the first things have passed away.
>
> *Revelation 21:4*

from the mortal to the immortal.

> We know that Christ being raised from the dead, will never die again; death no longer has dominion over him.
>
> *Romans 6:9*

And just as it is appointed for mortals to die once, and after that the judgment, so Christ, having been offered once to bear the sins of many, will appear a second time, not to deal with sin, but to save those who are eagerly waiting for him.

Hebrews 9:27, 28

Then, how can it not be good?

NOTES

1. The Psalmist was expressing the futility of even great strength from preventing death when he declares, "The war horse is a vain hope for victory, and by its great might it cannot save" (Psalms 33:17).

2. The Optimist's Prayer:

> As you ramble on through life, brother,
> Whatever may be your goal,
> Keep your eye upon the doughnut
> And not upon the hole.

3. Merlin offers immortality to King Arthur by presenting him the Holy Grail:

"Yes," the king's eyes flashed. "My life is important. To me. Because it is short and precious. Because each day may be my last. Because if I don't squeeze every drop of wonder from it I can, I will be forever diminished. That is why I am a good king, Merlin. That is why my life is worth living. Do you think I could bear to live through endless ages of endless days, knowing that there was no urgency to anything I did? Why, it would be worse than eternal Hell!"

"Those are personal considerations. Think of Britain."

"I do think of Britain, every moment. Britain needs many things, but what she doesn't need is some despot kept alive forever by sorcery to rule as he likes by whatever whim takes him at the moment."

"You wouldn't do that, Arthur."

"Oh, no? Not for the first hundred years, perhaps. Or two hundred—how long will you give me, anyway?"

Merlin made a dismissive gesture.

"One day I would bend, Merlin, as anyone would." His voice was very low. "And I would keep on bending until my soul was twisted and corrupt as a dead tree. No. I don't want it."

Molly Cochran and Warren Murphy, "The Forever King" (New York: TOR, 1992), p. 232.

LEAVING HERE . . .
GOING THERE
Death in Small Doses

During the summer after my first year of college, my entire seminary class was drafted into going to a summer camp for boys in the Allegheny Mountains. My classmate Harry and I were selected as counselors of a cabin for ten-year-olds. Harry was what we would today call a "Macho Man." He was a bodybuilder, weight lifter and an exercise enthusiast. He ran, swam, boxed, and rode horses. He was the ideal model of a counselor at a boys' camp. By comparison I was the ninety-five pound weakling who got sand kicked in his face at the beach. Harry would periodically tease me about my puny, physical condition and take great pride in the fact that he had never been sick a day in his life.

But, there was something Harry never figured on. He was an only child and I was the youngest of five.

What that translated into was that if there were any germs, diseases, or sicknesses around I invariably caught them. He, I surmised, must have lived in antiseptic conditions. Now, as anyone can tell you camps are hardly antiseptic, let alone a boys' camp. Besides, ten-year-olds are notorious for picking up all sorts of strange conditions from poison ivy to the plague. They are also renowned for sharing their diseases. So it happened that Harry got sick "for the first time in his life." I no longer recall what it was he caught from those generous donors but I can vividly remember how he reacted. Weeping and wailing, moaning and groaning doesn't come close to describing it. He wouldn't get out of bed, meals had to be brought to him, and he complained about everything from the camp nurse to the need for absolute quiet in the cabin. Even the kids recognized a crybaby when they saw one.

The point is that since Harry had never been sick before, his body had built up no resistance to illness. We develop immunity to many diseases by fighting them off while our bodies are young and healthy enough to withstand them. I have no doubt that it was that very observation that eventually led to the first vaccine. Vaccinations are nothing more than a weakened dose of the sickness given to us when we're healthy enough to combat it effectively and build up our immunity. Having confronted most if not all childhood diseases I was a walking immunity. While I may not have looked like much on the outside, I was just fine on the inside. Harry was beginning to learn one of life's more difficult lessons.

By the same token we can develop an immunity to death in the same way, that is, by taking weakened doses of it every now and then. Death is the ultimate "sickness" which we must all inevitably face. Yet, consider how society deals with it. Our first recourse is flight. There are many ways of fleeing death. We refuse to talk about it, we change the subject as soon as we can, we don't listen when it's brought up, or we beat a hasty exit. We also cosmetize death so that it will appear prettier than it is. How often do people comment at wakes at how "good" the corpse looks? We put deceased bodies in ornate and comfortable "beds." We surround them with flowers so that everything about death will look pretty as a picture. It's what I call a "deny and rely" response. Deny its reality and rely on your ingenuity to get around it. Nor have we helped our children to deal realistically or effectively with death. How can they when we don't? Death is unreal to children. It has no physical finality in their world. They see familiar faces die on television and in the movies only to reappear later in another film or series. Even violent or brutal death, to which they are subjected much too often in the media, lacks conviction. It is just simply fantasy.

If, however, we deal realistically with death in small doses whenever it arises we can begin to develop a healthy resistance to it. No soldier on the battlefield deals with death as a fantasy. Nor does a surgical nurse or a grief counselor. Yet, one need not have to deal with death with such repeated regularity in order to build up one's resistance. We must give each death that enters our life the attention it deserves, neither fleeing from it nor wallowing in it. It should be a time to share with family (old and young as well) and friends its meaning, its physical finality and spiritual implications. It is never something that should be passed over lightly or morosely. It's rather like getting your flu shots. They protect against this year's epidemic but you'll need another for next year's.

Actually, sickness is a lessened form of death, a sort of minideath. It is a rehearsal for the great performance. Someone once told me that life is a rehearsal for death. While I believe that life is a whole lot more, that is certainly an essential part of it. The better rehearsed we are, the better the chances for our performance.

As a young deacon giving adult religious instructions I was asked by a woman if being a good Christian meant not being afraid to die. Naively, I focused on the afterlife in the hopes that this would allay her fears. Her response was disarmingly appropriate. "It's not going there that bothers me," she said, "but, leaving here."

Only now do I begin to understand better what Jesus meant when he said "the kingdom of God is at hand."

Jesus was telling us that we don't have to wait to go "there." That "there" can be "here." That we can make the kingdom present in our midst by the way we believe and live. That if we don't do it here, how can we hope to find it there? Death is never overcome as if in some fantasy where the knight in shining armor rescues the damsel in distress from death's door at the last possible moment. Death in the Christian context is being constantly overcome, so that when Jesus comes "amid trumpet blasts on the clouds of heaven,"[1] it is not a surprise but something we've expected all along. He doesn't rescue us from death but instead leads us through it and past it. The truth is that if we have really lived our lives with Jesus we will have already tasted death many times before we die. As Shakespeare so aptly put it, "Cowards die many times before their death. The valiant tastes of death but once."[2] When we are so afraid of death, every little problem scares the life out of us. Every lump is cancer, every headache is a brain tumor, every sickness is fatal. Or we become overly obsessed with taking care of our bodies. We become "health nuts" to a fanatic degree by subjecting ourselves to an excessive regimen of daily, weekly, and monthly workouts, a growing consumption of vitamins and all kinds of other pills, an obsession with health foods and a Spartan, antiseptic lifestyle. It may all be just a subconscious flight from death, an outward manifestation of one's fear of dying. No fight, however, was ever won by fleeing.

Jesus faced death head-on. He touched the untouchables by laying healing hands upon them. He associated with the "unclean"[3] in order to cleanse them. He commiserated with the sick and cried over the dead. But, he never fled. Not even in the face of his own overwhelming death. The valiant tastes of death but once.

Christians who follow in his footsteps will have so strengthened their own resistance to death that they, too, will have become immune to it. Then, they will shout with Saint Paul, "O, death where is your victory? Where is your sting?"[4]

NOTES

1. 1 Thessalonians 4:16–17.
2.   Cowards die many times before their deaths;
       The valiant never taste of death but once. . . .
       It seems to me most strange that men should fear;
       Seeing that death, a necessary end,
       Will come when it will come.
                          Julius Caesar II, ii, 32–37

3. In Jesus' time lepers were required to call out "unclean" if they approached those who were clean.
4. 1 Corinthians 15:55.

· 3 ·

TWO GLASSES OF WATER

*Y*oung people today are assaulted by changing values at a rate faster than at any other time in history. Television, movies, radio, and records bombard
then with options heretofore unheard-of. Somewhere
in the maelstrom old and traditional values are fast becoming lost. It is no wonder when you consider how
much of their time is consumed by the media and how
much by religion. It is a fair statement to say that children and adolescents spend about the equivalent of a
work week, forty hours every week inundated, edu-
cated, shaped, and formed by the media and perhaps
one to two hours indoctrinated by their church. Even
then such "church time" is usually submitted to, at
best. More often than not it is met with opposition,
even hostility. Hardly an attitude conducive to learn-
ing. Besides, the competition is better trained, less restrained, and economically well maintained. Which
explains my reluctance when asked to speak to the stu-
dent body of a local boys' high school about sin.

It would be an understatement to say that Daniel faced the lions' den with more assurance than I did that crowd. Would I have the courage Daniel did in confronting a raging mob?[1] Would I have the inspired wisdom he had to set them aright? As I prepared for that fatal confrontation my mouth became so dry that even repeated glasses of water failed to alleviate the problem. Then it struck me that the glass in my hand was offering me a possible solution as did the potter's wheel for Jeremiah.[2]

When, at last, the fateful time arrived and the assembly settled down I placed on the podium two glasses of water, one disgustingly dirty and the other crystal clear. "I set before you a choice," I said.[3] I went on to explain that the clear glass of water was simply that and nothing more. It would possibly slake one's thirst at very best. The dirty glass on the other hand contained all manner of foul things from cigarette butts and ashes to gutter sludge. Still in spite of the many awful things I had thrown into it I also put in several shots of assorted liquors which I had brought along.

"This glass while it contains contaminated water will give you a buzz if you drink it. It's got a zing to it," I declared. "Now, the choice is yours. The clean water or the dirty water?"

I waited a brief moment for the challenge to sink in and then hastily added, "Before you make your choice however, I think it's only fair to warn you that if you

drink the dirty water it will *most surely kill you!*
Now decide."

The scoffing and derision were instantaneous.
"What do you think we are—stupid?" "Let our teach-
ers drink the dirty water. We'll take the clean water."

This was their moment and I let them have it unin-
terrupted. When they settled down somewhat I said,
"The truth is that all of us will eventually choose the
dirty water."

We've been doing it since we were first confronted
with that decision. It was the choice God gave Adam
and Eve in the Garden.

> And the LORD God commanded the man,
> "You may freely eat of every tree of the gar-
> den; But of the tree of the knowledge of good
> and evil you shall not eat, for in the day that
> you eat of it you shall die."
>
> *Genesis 2:16-17*

They chose wrong. So did their children and their children's children. And so do we. But, here's the incred-
ible part. When things go wrong, as we are warned
they will if we drink the dirty water, we blame it on
God. We get sick and we blame God. We die and we
blame God. Then we say, "How can this loving and
good God do this to us?"

The Scriptures constantly remind us that we are do-

ing it to ourselves! We choose death and then blame
God for the consequences of our choice. If God did
not warn us, and repeatedly through a long succession
of prophets, then God would not be a God of love.
But, God did and still we blame God.

Just as Adam and Eve had the freedom to eat of all
the trees of the Garden and chose the forbidden fruit
for the apparent zing it offered,

> So when the woman saw that the tree was
> good for food, and that it was a delight to the
> eyes, and that the tree was to be desired to
> make one wise, she took of its fruit and ate;
> and she also gave some to her husband, who
> was with her, and he ate.
>
> *Genesis 3:6*

So, too, have we done the same. We are surrounded
with good. When we choose the bad we suffer the
consequences of that choice. Why then do we blame
God? Why, when God warned us from the very
beginning?

The wonder of it all is not that we die but that our
choice of the dirty water has not undone us. This loving God is merciful. We were not left to wallow in our
plight. God has sent someone to save us from our folly.
A savior. What was lost in Paradise can be recaptured.

However, the Garden of Eden is no longer a place . . .
but a person—Jesus Christ.

NOTES

1. The boy Daniel challenged a lynch mob determined to stone
   the innocent Susanna, falsely accused of adultery, by trip-
   ping up her accusers with a clever ploy (Daniel 13).
2. Jeremiah was inspired while watching a potter at his wheel
   to draw an analogy about God and Israel (Jeremiah 18:1ff).
3. In the desert Moses offered the Israelites a choice between
   life and death (Deuteronomy 30:19).

GOD DID NOT MAKE DEATH

God did not make death, and he does not
delight in the death of the living.

Wisdom 1:13

God did not make death! If I had my way I
would have that flashing in neon lights twenty-
four hours a day in front of every church throughout
the world. If I had my way I would have it emblazoned
over every funeral parlor and cemetery in every country throughout the world. If I had my way I would
have it inscribed in stone at the entrance of every hos-
pital, convalescent home, infirmary, and old folks'
home throughout the world. God did not make death.[1]
If I had my way I would have all believers repeat the
phrase seven times seventy times a day like a mantra
or sung antiphonally every morning, noon, and night.
For some strange reason I don't believe people know
it, or if they do, they don't seem to believe it.

I assert this because of the way most people speak

about death. When referring to the tragic death of children I have countless times heard people say that God took them while they were still very young. If the intent is to be consoling, and I have every reason to believe that it is, it falls pitifully short of the mark. God does not lie in wait to take anyone, let alone children. God did not make death.

At the untimely death of an adult, I have heard people say, "God called her in the prime of her life." God is not some sort of grim reaper waiting to call anyone to death. How can he when Wisdom reminds us that God did not make death?

When confronted with a suffering old person, I have heard people say, "It would be better if God were to come and get her," or, "It would be merciful for God to take him." God does not call anyone to death or take anyone by death. God did not make death. When God calls anyone, it is to life. When God takes anyone anywhere, it is to live. Our God is a god of the living, not of the dead. If you think it is more merciful for an older person to die (and it may be) then don't call on God. God only brings life. Pray that Death may come quickly and mercifully. Then pray that God will come at the same moment to bring new life, resurrected life.

Pious sounding phrases don't always convey the proper truth. To say, "The Lord giveth and the Lord taketh away," at someone's death is to seriously misquote Job who was talking about material goods and not life and death.[2] Think of what we might otherwise be implying. If God's call could bring life or death, people would have only a fifty-fifty chance of living through it. Hardly what I would call appealing odds.

The question then is, "What about death?" Where did it come from? Why do people die? Whose fault is it?

There are any number of reasons why we die. For one, we are not perfect. Only God is perfect. That is tantamount to saying that it is inevitable that we will all break down. For another thing, we were made of the stuff of the earth.[3] Flesh is not immortal. We have only to look around to see that. All living flesh eventually dies. The body is not immortal in spite of all our wishes and efforts to the contrary. Still again, if human bodies were immortal, where on earth would we all fit after so many generations have passed since Adam and Eve? We would be standing one on top of the other more than five dozen deep by now.

Nevertheless, none of that answers the philosophical/theological question. The Book of Wisdom does explain just a few verses later.

> But through the devil's envy death entered the world. . . .
>
> *Wisdom 2:24a*

When confronted with the question, Jesus answered it in parable.

> Another parable he put before them, saying, "The kingdom of heaven may be compared

to a man who sowed good seed in his field; but while men were sleeping, his enemy came and sowed weeds among the wheat, and went away. So when the plants came up and bore grain, then the weeds appeared also. And the servants of the householder came and said to him, 'Sir, did you not sow good seed in your field? How then has it weeds?' He said to them, 'An enemy has done this.' The servants said to him, 'Then do you want us to go and gather them?' But he said, 'No; lest in gathering the weeds you root up the wheat along with them. Let both grow together until the harvest; and at harvest time I will tell the reapers, Gather the weeds first and bind them in bundles to be burned, but gather the wheat into my barn.'"

(Italics mine) Matthew 13:25–30

God did not make death. God brings life. We might all too quickly claim that if we were God we would do away with death, all death, even the smaller deaths—sickness, pain, or suffering. How then would humanity deal with all the problems that would surely follow? While we eliminate the weed, we might also be cutting down the wheat. It is for us who were made in the image of God to be like God and act as Jesus did, bringing life wherever we go. We must not become so preoccupied with the weeds that we fail to take proper care of the wheat. We have all seen those who are so obsessed with casting out demons that seven worse ones hasten to fill the vacuum just as Jesus warned.[4] We have also watched those who were so preoccupied with not dying that they have lost the joy of living. Jesus' advice still stands. Let the weeds and the wheat grow together. We are to attend to the wheat. To act lovingly and sacrificially whenever we encounter suffering, pain, problems, or difficulties. To bring comfort and solace in the face of every little or big death. To be like God—life bearers.

In giving we expand our own capacity to bring life. Jesus healed the bleeding woman and eventually the dead child. We will be able to perform the works of Christ and more.

> Very truly, I tell you, the one who believes in me will also do the works that I do and, in fact, will do greater works than these, because I am going to the Father.
>
> *John 14:12*

There is good in suspending physical sickness and even physical death. But, it must not stop here. It must never end here. What good is it to heal the mortal body and not provide for the immortal soul? As precious as the wheat plant is, its purpose is served only when it brings forth the kernel of wheat.

At harvest time the wheat will be gathered into barns

and saved. All the harvesters will rejoice. And death will be no more.

> He will wipe every tear from their eyes. Death will be no more; mourning and crying and pain will be no more, for the first things have passed away.
>
> *Revelation 21:4*

NOTES

1. Or, for that matter, its smaller version—sickness.
2. Job 1:21.
3. Genesis 2:7.
4. Matthew 12:45.

LIFE

· 5 ·

A MATTER OF TIME

*F*or us life passes minute by minute. There is a past, a present, and a future. What is past is irretrievably gone and what is future is unknown and unknowable. All we have is right *now*.

It is a fluid *now* however, for even as we say it, it passes. There is no way for us to grab hold of it and keep it from getting away from us. We cannot freeze the present moment except in a photograph. We cannot stop time except in our imagination.

This is what we call human time. It is not the same with God. God's time is not the same as our time. It is a whole other dimension, a different reality. It is a reality that is difficult to express since we cannot know it directly, that is, from our own experience. God lives in our time but somehow outside of it, apart from it or above it. What this means simply is that there is no past or future in God. There is just the present with God. God sees only *now*. But, God's *now* takes in everything—our past, present, and future in one broad sweep.

We might compare it to a microdot. While it appears as no more than a speck of ink, closer examination reveals that there can be what would amount to pages and pages of material contained in it. God sees the entire cosmic history of the universe, countless trillions of years long, as a microdot moment. Many people who have come out of near-death experiences *(nde)*[1] say that during that time their whole life "flashed" before them. They experienced not only the aggregate sum of their lives but even the individual and separate parts with their own special feelings and sensations.[2] Present technology gives us even newer ways of expressing this. It's like an entire videotape played in fast forward but it takes only an instant to do so.

Consequently, what God sees is all of history in a flash, a moment—now. Our past can never be lost to God since it is always just happening. At this very moment God is watching us being born, cutting our first tooth, starting our first day in school, going on a first date, getting married, and so on. How can God forget if He is watching it happen right now? How can God forget what He's seeing while He's seeing it? Even if a mother should forget the child of her womb, God tells Isaiah, I will never forget you.

> But Zion said, "The LORD has forsaken me, my Lord has forgotten me." Can a woman forget her nursing child, or show no compassion for the child of her womb? Even these

may forget, yet I will not forget you. See, I
have inscribed you on the palms of my hands;
your walls are continually before me.[3]

So also is our future happening right now before God.
God is not foretelling the future. God is watching the
future taking place. We cannot surprise God about
what we will do later on because God is watching it
happen right now.

This is why God is pictured as the all-seeing eye.
The following illustration may help to understand this
important concept.

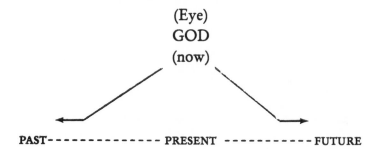

While we live in the time line of past, present, and
future, God sees it all in one grand sweep. This concept
becomes extremely important to understanding life-
after-death experiences. If the transition from death to
resurrection means a passage from human time into
God's time, then at the moment of death we enter the

eternal now of God. Eternity is not a trillion years or a billion trillion years. It is not a succession in time. It is a moment that stretches forever in both directions—past and future. When we enter death we enter the moment. In God we are present to all time.

NOTES

1. Those who were considered clinically dead and then came back to life again. Commonly abbreviated *nde*.
2. Cf. Raymond A. Moody, Jr., *Life after Life* (New York: Bantam, 1986); Margot Grey, *Return from Death: An Exploration of the Near Death Experience* (Boston and London: Arkana, 1985); Margot Grey, *Other World Experiences*, et al.
3. Isaiah 49:14–16.

· 6 ·

PRECIOUS BODY

One afternoon I got a call at the rectory that the son of former parishioners of mine had died in a tragic accident at work. Just twenty-five-years old, his young life had been cut short when a truck he had been working on crushed him. As I drove to the house I remembered the time when Jim was a rambunctious teenager and his mother brought him to my office for a "good talking to." He was really no different from all other boys his age, it was just that he was the oldest child and this was their first encounter with adolescent rebellion. Somehow we all made it through that time and a few other times. When he made it into young adulthood, we all heaved a collective sigh of relief. Now, just as his parents were beginning to reap the fruits of their labor, his life came to a sudden and tragic end.

I offered as much consolation as any friend could, having long since learned that very little of what is said at such times impacts as much as simple, loving presence. The following day when I arrived at the funeral parlor I was met at the door by Jim's dad. "She's taking it really bad," he said trying to prepare me for what lay ahead. When I entered the viewing room Margaret was leaning over the coffin holding onto Jim's cold, lifeless hand. "She won't let go of him," he said with tear-filled eyes. "We've all tried but she won't let go."

I went over to her knowing that I could not minimize her grief but prayed that I could bring her some hope at such a desolate time. I spoke as gently as I could about resurrection and letting go, when she disarmed me by giving one of the greatest testimonials of human love I had ever heard. "I know my Jimmy's dead," she sobbed. "I can accept that as difficult as it is. I just don't want them to take him away from me where I will never see him again. I would take him even dead if I could just see him and touch him every now and then."

Driving back to the parish I understood human love better than I ever had in my entire life. This body is precious. Not only precious but holy, sacred, and wonderful. What a remarkable revelation. I had been raised to think of the body as the enemy. Since my early seminary days as an adolescent I had been taught to fight against the desires and impulses of the body, that the body was at war with the spirit. The body must be denied, disciplined, and subdued. Even today I can't escape the feeling that giving in to the body in whatever way is somehow wrong or sinful. That somehow holiness is inescapably tied up with "body-lessness."

What a terrible misconception! What an affront to the goodness of all God's creation. What an implicit rejection of the incarnation of God in Jesus. We have made an enemy of the very vehicle of our exaltation and transformation.

Consider if you will that God had an entire universe, an entire creation to choose from when he decided to get into it, intimate with it. God could have picked any order of being for the Second Person of the Trinity to become—an angel, an extraterrestrial, any animal, or even a heavenly body. Instead of incarnation it could have been "inangelation" or "inplanetation." The point is that there was something about human beings that appealed to God more than all the rest.

> What are human beings that you are mindful
> of them, mortals that you care for them? Yet
> you have made them a little lower than God,
> and crowned them with glory and honor.
> *Psalms 8:4–5*

The body is an essential part of being a human being. God did not choose to become an angel, a planet, or a star. If the body is essential to being who we are and what we are then it is essential in our salvation and our resurrection. How can we hate the body and not hate the incarnation of God? It is in the body where "God and Man at table are sat down."[1]

God loves the body as it is, as a fully human body, with its biology, psychology, sexuality, and idiosyncrasies. The love song says, "Don't change your hair for me, not if you care for me." Considering all that we go through for the sake of human love—dieting, dressing, exercising, painting, plucking, scenting, fixing—it's refreshing and rewarding to know that none of that is necessary to gain God's love. We already have it without that. We may not love one another for any number of body reasons but in that regard we can be assured that God's love for us is unconditional.[2] One of the most touching examples of this, as we have seen, is the love of a mother for the child of her womb. Isaiah, we remember, heralds this sentiment and relates it to God.

> But Zion said, "The LORD has forsaken me, my Lord has forgotten me." Can a woman forget her nursing child, or show no compassion for the child of her womb? Even these may forget, yet I will not forget you.
>
> *Isaiah 49:14–15*

If God considers the body so precious that it was His/Her object of choice, should we not also hold it precious? While the body is not God it is the vessel that holds God. It is the treasure house for God-touching experiences, the temple of God. Wanting to hold onto something that is so precious in the sight of God is not wrong or idolatrous but ultimately a veiled desire to hold onto God Himself/Herself.

When Margaret wanted to hold on to Jimmy and not let go it was her way of expressing what God expressed in the resurrection of Jesus—the promised continuation of this very precious body. We will not have to let go of the body. For the first time in my life I began to understand Christianity's reverence for relics, especially in its early history. Initially, the practice was neither idolatrous, superstitious, nor foolish, although it did degenerate later. If we save and store precious stones, then why not precious bones? A lock of my mother's hair is far more precious to me than diamonds or pearls. Celebrating eucharist in the catacombs was the early Christians' way of affirming life and afterlife in the very midst of death. When they emerged from the tombs they carried the bones of their loved ones with them and celebrated over them lest they forget. If God can count our hairs and number our bones, should we find it abhorrent?

And even the hairs of your head are all counted.

Matthew 10:30

Many are the afflictions of the righteous, but the LORD rescues them from them all. He

keeps all their bones; not one of them will
be broken.

Psalms 34:19–20

A woman told me that after the burial of her husband, her children told her that it was time to move
on with life. To get her to do this they gave away all
his personal effects. Later she discovered that the last
undershirt he wore was in the clothes hamper and had
been missed. She hid it from her children and never
told them about it. "Every now and then when the
memories become really strong and irresistible," she
said, "I take it out of its hiding place and bury my face
in it. You know," she continued, emotionally caught
up in her confession, "even after all these years I can
still faintly smell the aroma of him there and for a while
I feel he is with me again."

Should this be dismissed as maudlin sentimentality?
Of course, we must continue on with life but does that
mean we have to eradicate from our lives all vestiges
of what was once so very cherished and special? Jesus
said to Mary Magdalene, "Don't hold me back."[3] He
and the deceased must move on to the fullness of resurrection. But we are not left without the consoling, continued "physical" presence of Christ even if in a "new
form,"[4] a form Christians would later call sacramental.

NOTES

1. Folk song, from People's Mass Book.

2. We may not feel so confident in other areas even though the same holds true.
3. Jesus said to her, "Do not hold on to me, because I have not yet ascended to the Father. But go to my brothers and say to them, 'I am ascending to my Father and your Father, to my God and your God'" (John 20:17).
4. "He will give a new form to this lowly body of ours and remake it according to the pattern of his glorified body" (Philippians 3:21). This statement becomes immensely important to understanding life-after-death experiences, as will be explained in later chapters.

FOREVER MOMENTS

*A*ll of us have experienced times in our lives that were so precious and special that if it were possible we would have had time stand still so that we might live that moment forever. If we could have we would have grabbed hold of it with both hands and never let it go. Very special times like graduation day, first date, wedding day, a family Christmas, honeymoon, birth of a child. The list could go on and on.

One day while I was at the diocesan office building a receptionist told me that she had recently been at a friend's party and while watching home movies saw a brief segment on their grade-school graduation. You cannot imagine my surprise when she told me that I was in those movies. I had a few precious snapshots of that time but I had absolutely no recollection of anyone having taken movies. Nobody I knew in 1951 had a motion-picture camera. She assured me it was no mistake and promised to get the film for me.

When I sat and watched it a flood of deep and rich nostalgia overtook me. There were my classmates, the girls and boys I had spent eight years of my life with, most of whom I have not seen since, the way they were, the way I remembered them. None of us had grown old. None of us had changed. As I sat there I was feeling once again the same, tremendous happiness I so obviously expressed in the film as the camera panned back and forth over us. Watching those few precious moments on film was like being transported back into time where "then" suddenly became "now" and I was thirteen years old once more. I had the same toothless grin, the same familiar slouch and the same incessantly chattering mouth. Then all too soon, it ended. I immediately played it again and then over and over again, but the more I did the more I began to lose it. The forever moment was gone.

Kodak tells us to "capture the moment!" It is something we all want to do. It is something deep within us that refuses to let go of the good times. Why should we? After all, a good time is a taste of God and since God is forever, why not the good times?

Unfortunately, nothing we do this side of heaven is forever. We are temporal, which means we are temporary and therefore everything passes. The soul inside us rejects our temporality. After all, *it* is immortal. But, not the body. It is not immortal. At least, not the way it is. But, the body speaks in the physical world what it knows and believes in the spiritual. The body tries to grab on to immortality, hold it, and never let it go. It produces offspring, it builds lasting monuments, it writes its name on stone. Nonetheless, plagues and wars wipe out dynasties, pyramids crumble, and gravestone inscriptions fade with the passing years.

Nothing we do lasts forever. Only God is forever. If we wish to grab hold of forever we must grab hold of God. The wonder is that humanity was able to grab hold of God and never let go. We did it in Jesus. Jesus is our forever moment.

AFTERLIFE

Resurrection

· 8 ·

HE IS NOT HERE!

*I*t is Sunday morning. Jesus had been hastily buried after his death because of Jewish regulations regarding the Sabbath. With sunrise the Sabbath ended so Mary Magdalene came to the tomb to anoint his body with funeral ointment. She was stunned to find that the tomb was open and the body of her beloved Jesus was gone. Her concern was not why it was done, several possibilities came to mind immediately, but who could have done it. The Gospel account states:

> Meanwhile Mary stood weeping outside the tomb. As she wept, she bent over to look into the tomb, and she saw two angels in white, sitting where the body of Jesus had been lying, one at the head and the other at the feet. They said to her, "Woman, why are you weeping?" She said to them, "They have taken away my Lord, and I do not know where they have laid him." When she had said this, she turned around and saw Jesus stand-

ing there, *but she did not know that it was Jesus.* Jesus said to her, "Woman, why are you weeping? Whom are you looking for?" Supposing him to be the gardener, she said to him, "Sir, if you have carried him away, tell me where you have laid him, and I will take him away.

(Italics mine) John 20:11–15

How could this be? How could someone as close to Jesus as Mary Magdalene not recognize him? She had been with him for the better part of his public ministry, had accompanied him and the disciples along with the other women taking care of their daily needs, and even stuck by him to the very end at the foot of the cross. Now, barely more than a full day later she looks him in the face and has no idea who this man is that's talking to her. She thinks he's the gardener. How can this be? How can anyone read this and not wonder, "Was it really Jesus?"

The disciples on the road to Emmaus were very close followers of Jesus, very likely in the inner circle. They had to have been in order for them to have known on that very same Sunday all the intimate details about his resurrection. We can also assume from the Gospel account that they had been at the miracle of the multiplication of the loaves. These were no casual observers. Now follow their encounter with the resurrected Jesus.

Now on that same day two of them were going to a village called Emmaus, about seven
miles from Jerusalem, and talking with each
other about all these things that had happened. While they were talking and discussing, Jesus himself came near and went
with them, *but their eyes were kept from recognizing him.*

(Italics mine) Luke 24:13–16

Once again close friends of Jesus did not recognize
him after he resurrected. As the account continues we
see that this was no brief encounter. Jesus walks along
with them, has a lively discussion with them, and even
joins them for dinner. They had to have heard Jesus
teach countless times before and yet they did not even
recognize his voice! How could this be? It has to leave
you wondering if they were deceived. Was it really
him?

Then again, none of these were Apostles. If anyone,
the Apostles should know Jesus if they were to see him
and hear him.

After these things Jesus showed himself again
to the disciples by the Sea of Tiberias; and he
showed himself in this way. Gathered there
together were Simon Peter, Thomas called the
Twin, Nathanael of Cana in Galilee, the sons
of Zebedee, and two others of his disciples.

> Simon Peter said to them, "I am going fish-
> ing." They said to him, "We will go with
> you." They went out and got into the boat,
> but that night they caught nothing. Just after
> daybreak, Jesus stood on the beach; *but the
> disciples did not know that it was Jesus.*
> (*Italics mine*) *John 21:1–4*

Seven. Count them. Seven of the remaining eleven Apostles were there looking at Jesus and talking to him but they did not know who it was. Now this is certainly a puzzlement. They had already encountered the resurrected Jesus in the upper room at Jerusalem. Why did they not recognize him in Galilee? Even while Jesus is eating breakfast with them, they still weren't quite sure.

> Jesus said to them, "Come and have break-
> fast." Now none of the disciples dared to ask
> him, "Who are you?"
> *John 21:12*

Something is terribly wrong here. How can one read these Gospel accounts of the resurrection of Jesus and not wonder if, in fact, he really did resurrect. As it turns out, these very accounts have caused many to deny the validity of Jesus' resurrection or at the very best to assert his spiritual rather than his bodily resurrection. For anyone to have studied the Gospels and claim to have never doubted does no credit to the Gospels or one's faith. Thomas himself doubted. Doubting is not a sin. Nor does it denote a lack of faith. Lack of faith is a pure and simple disbelief. Doubting is an invitation to enter into the mystery more deeply, to go beyond the superficial. If the Gospel writers were trying to perpetrate a fraud, as some claim, why would they relate the accounts in a way that would be sure to raise doubts? They could have retold the stories definitively and unquestionably. Liars do not set obvious traps for themselves. The fact that the resurrection narratives raise doubts is more an argument for their veracity than their fraudulence.

Once that issue is settled in our minds and our hearts are at ease, we can proceed. Stated simply, the people in Jesus' time were having difficulty with resurrection. Why?

· 9 ·

BODILY EXPECTATIONS

*R*esurrection was not a new idea at the time of
Jesus. The Gospel tells us that it was a hotly de-
bated issue. Saint Paul threw the Jewish court, the
Sanhedrin, into a quandary at the mere mention of it
(Acts 22:30ff). Like today there were those who believed and those who didn't. But, even for those who
believed there was no clear understanding of what it
might mean. Ezekiel talks about skeleton bones coming together again.

> Then he said to me, "Prophesy to these
> bones, and say to them: O dry bones, hear
> the word of the LORD. Thus says the LORD
> GOD to these bones: I will cause breath to
> enter you, and you shall live. I will lay sinews
> on you, and will cause flesh to come upon
> you, and cover you with skin, and put breath
> in you, and you shall live; and you shall know
> that I am the LORD."
>
> *Ezekiel 37:4–6*

Elijah and Elisha had brought young men back to life.

> But he said to her, "Give me your son." He took him from her bosom, carried him up into the upper chamber where he was lodging, and laid him on his own bed. He cried out to the LORD, "O LORD my God, have you brought calamity even upon the widow with whom I am staying, by killing her son?" Then he stretched himself upon the child three times, and cried out to the LORD, "O LORD my God, let this child's life come into him again." The LORD listened to the voice of Elijah; the life of the child came into him again, and he revived.
>
> *1 Kings 17:20–22*

> When Elisha came into the house, he saw the child lying dead on his bed. So he went in and closed the door on the two of them, and prayed to the LORD. Then he got up on the bed and lay upon the child, putting his mouth upon his mouth, his eyes upon his eyes, and his hands upon his hands; and while he lay bent over him, the flesh of the child became warm. He got down, walked once to and fro in the room, then got up again and bent over

him; the child sneezed seven times, and the
child opened his eyes.

2 Kings 4:32–35

The Gospels tell us about Jesus' raising from the
dead Jairus's daughter, the son of the widow of Nain
and Lazarus. There is certainly ample evidence in
Scripture of the dead being brought back to life, but
is that resurrection or resuscitation?

Everyone agrees that these are examples of resuscitation, that is, this body as it is comes back to life again.
An example of this might be someone restored to
breathing by mouth-to-mouth resuscitation or someone who drowned in ice water is restored to life hours
later. Resuscitation happened in the past and continues
to happen with even greater frequency in our day.
However, this is not what is meant by resurrection.

Resurrection means that our bodies as they are, are
irrevocably and irretrievably dead, and still we come
back. The fact that most people in thinking about resurrection conjure up images of bodily resuscitation is
understandable since we lack experiences of any other
kind. Besides, this was no doubt the expectation in the
time of Jesus and it continues to be the option of choice
today in books and movies.

Such a fixed mind-set only serves to confuse the issue. If we're looking for it to happen one way and
something else occurs we don't know what we're dealing with. It's a credit to the honesty of the Evangelists

that they recorded the resurrection accounts as faithfully as they did considering the dubiousness of the eyewitness accounts. But, rather than impose our expectations on the matter, should we not be more objective and try to understand what actually did happen? After all, as far as Christians are concerned this is the first-ever account of resurrection in history. Instead of saying how it should be, let's examine and learn from how it actually was.

· 10 ·

A NEW REALITY

*T*he fact is that resurrection is a new reality. Since the earliest beginnings of human history there has been evidence of belief in life after death. How it took place and where it took place were and remain mysteries. But, the belief that it takes place is always present. Bodies were buried with tools and food to support the departed in the next life. Tombs of the pharaohs were equipped with boats to carry them back and forth from this life to the other one. Chinese emperors were buried with armies to protect them in the afterlife. Spirits of dead ancestors in India come back in sacred cows. Reincarnation has people returning again and again as humans, butterflies, deer, and any number of other animals. Of course, there's the age-old favorite— ghosts. The strange thing is that the belief has persisted over countless thousands of years in spite of the absence of hard evidence to support it. Can this be pure fiction? Can fifty million Frenchmen be wrong? Or a hundred billion humans for that matter?

I think not. What all of this is saying is that we don't

know how we will come back but we're definitely coming back. Life is not over at our death. Or as the preface for the Mass of the Dead proclaims, "Life is not ended—only changed." This is simply restating what Saint Paul wrote to the Philippeans:

> He will give a new form to this lowly body of ours.
>
> *Philippians 3:21*

Since Paul went about preaching the resurrection of Jesus it was natural for people to ask how it was to take place. He deals with this issue in his letter to the Corinthians.

> But someone will ask, "How are the dead raised? With what kind of body do they come?" Fool! What you sow does not come to life unless it dies. And as for what you sow, you do not sow the body that is to be . . . So it is with the resurrection of the dead. What is sown is perishable, what is raised is imperishable.
>
> *1 Corinthians 15:35–37, 42*

That's about as much light as he sheds on the mystery in spite of the fact that his only encounter with Jesus was with the resurrected Jesus. It would have been helpful if he had been more specific. Could he have been? Or was he being deliberately evasive?

The German theologian Helmut Thielicke tells a story about two medieval monks discussing death. They promised one another that whoever died first would return the next night and, in reply to the question *Qualiter?* ("What's it like?"), answer either *Taliter* ("Same"—as we thought) or *Aliter* ("Other"—than we imagined). Finally, one of the monks died. The next evening he appeared as a ghost to his brother monk, who asked anxiously, *"Qualiter?"* To which came the answer, *"Totaliter aliter!"* ("Totally different!").

What is all of this saying? First, that this body will die and not come back exactly as it is (resuscitation). Second, that the resurrected body will take on a new and imperishable form. Third, that we want to remain in some form of contact with the deceased. Fourth, how their returnings and communications with us take place are not always clear or obvious. Finally and most importantly, we have a persistent and undeniable belief in life after death, as well as a belief that we can still have some form of contact with those who have died, regardless of a lack of hard evidence and scientific proof.

· 11 ·

A PATTERN
IN RESURRECTION

*I*t seems obvious then, that what we are looking for is not what we can expect. The great escape artist Harry Houdini, who was obsessed with contacting his mother after she died, told his wife that if there was a way to come back after his own death, he would find it. Although she tried faithfully to communicate with him for years and still others also tried after her death, no contact has been made. One would presume that if anyone could have found a way back, the Great Houdini would have.

Or were they all looking in the wrong places? Could their search have been frustrated like the search for the purloined letter in Edgar Allan Poe's story because what they were looking for was hiding in plain sight? Expectations have a way of blinding us to other possibilities.

Since the only account we have of resurrection is that of Jesus', perhaps we should examine more closely what actually happened and without prejudice. On first reading we are simply happy about the fact of resurrection. That's all we're interested in, so that's all we hear. On second reading, we may become a little uneasy about the conflicting stories and the lack of recognition of the resurrected Jesus, so we pass over it quickly so as not to disturb our faith. Besides, it's something we want to believe in, to say nothing about being loyal to our Christian faith. Once we get past these prejudices and can study the Gospels to see what they are actually telling us, I believe we will see a pattern emerging in all the resurrection accounts.

What the Gospels state quite explicitly and unquestionably is that Jesus died.

> Then Jesus cried again with a loud voice and breathed his last.
> *Matthew 27:50*

> Then Jesus gave a loud cry and breathed his last.
> *Mark 15:37*

> Then Jesus, crying with a loud voice, said, "Father, into your hands I commend my spirit." Having said this, he breathed his last.
> *Luke 23:46*

> When Jesus had received the wine, he said,

"It is finished." Then he bowed his head and gave up his spirit.

John 19:30

Lest there should be any doubt, John's Gospel makes assurance doubly sure.

> Since it was the day of Preparation, the Jews did not want the bodies left on the cross during the Sabbath, especially because that Sabbath was a day of great solemnity. So they asked Pilate to have the legs of the crucified men broken and the bodies removed. Then the soldiers came and broke the legs of the first and of the other who had been crucified with him. But when they came to Jesus and saw that he was already dead, they did not break his legs. Instead, one of the soldiers pierced his side with a spear, and at once blood and water came out.
>
> *John 19:31–34*

There must have been doubters and skeptics even back then because the Evangelist felt the necessity to add this additional parenthetical comment:

(He who saw this has testified so that you

also may believe. His testimony is true, and
he knows that he tells the truth.)

John 19:35

How anyone could have endured the brutality of a
crucifixion, the most cruel form of punishment ever
devised, after suffering from beatings, whippings,
crowning with thorns, and carrying a cross, and not
have died defies credibility. Add to that the piercing
with a lance from which blood and eventually water
flowed and there can be no doubt about it. Jesus was
dead.

Next, when the resurrected Jesus appeared, he was
not recognized. Mary Magdalene thought he was a gardener. The disciples on the road to Emmaus took him
for a stranger. The Apostles at the Sea of Galilee were
afraid to ask him who he was. What the accounts are
saying rather explicitly is that resurrection appearances
are not readily identifiable as such. Perhaps it's because
we have other preferential ones in mind, like resusci-
tated bodies or ghosts. But, whatever the reason, resurrection experiences seem to catch us off guard. This
should be no surprise since the Scriptures show us time
and again how God has to catch us off guard in order
to get a word in edgewise. Prejudices can impede truth.
Resurrection experiences are not usually how we expect them or when we expect them.

Then, something happens to spark recognition.

Otherwise, how would they have known that it was Jesus if it neither looked nor sounded like him?

> Jesus said to her, "Woman, why are you weeping? Whom are you looking for?" Supposing him to be the gardener, she said to him, "Sir, if you have carried him away, tell me where you have laid him, and I will take him away." Jesus said to her, "Mary!" She turned and said to him in Hebrew, "Rabbouni!" (which means Teacher).
>
> *John 20:15–16*

The moment she heard Jesus call her by name she knew who it was! Even though it didn't look or sound like him. This might seem far-fetched except for two things. It's not just that you say my name *but the way you say it* that's important. Ask any people who are close and intimate friends. There is a certain identifiable quality in the way that we say things. Also, Jesus may have called her in a way that we might describe today as a "pet" name, the way one might call Mary "Mare." The reason I say this is because Mary responds not by calling him "Rabbi," the more common form of address but the unusual, "Rabbouni." Was that her pet name for him? "Teach?"

The disciples on the road had no idea that it was Jesus who was accompanying them. Then something happened to spark recognition.

When he was at the table with them, he took bread, blessed and broke it, and gave it to them. Then their eyes were opened, and they recognized him.

Luke 24:30–31

In spite of the fact that Jesus had spoken to them at length the way he had in the past, it was not until he broke bread in that somehow familiar way that "their eyes were opened." That was obviously what triggered their recognition. They must have seen Jesus do this in the past and in just the same way for them to have responded so quickly to it. Had they been at the multiplication of the loaves in the desert? Had they sat at table with him enough times to have the gesture become the sign of the man? How could it have been otherwise?

At the Sea of Galilee the Apostles were out fishing all night but had caught nothing. Suddenly at daybreak, a stranger calls out to them. They obviously have no idea who it was or they would have responded to him immediately. Jesus talks to them but they still have no idea who it is. Finally, he does something and they realize that it's him.

Just after daybreak, Jesus stood on the beach; but the disciples did not know that it was Jesus. Jesus said to them, "Children, you have no fish, have you?" They answered him,

"No." He said to them, "Cast the net to the right side of the boat, and you will find some." So they cast it, and now they were not able to haul it in because there were so many fish. That disciple whom Jesus loved said to Peter, "It is the Lord!"

John 21:4–7

Does the incident sound familiar? It's identical to what happened at the beginning of Jesus' public ministry.

When he had finished speaking, he said to Simon, "Put out into the deep water and let down your nets for a catch." Simon answered, "Master, we have worked all night long but have caught nothing. Yet if you say so, I will let down the nets." When they had done this, they caught so many fish that their nets were beginning to break. So they signaled their partners in the other boat to come and help them. And they came and filled both boats, so that they began to sink.

Luke 5:4–7

If it's familiar to us, imagine how familiar it must have been to them. Even though this stranger did not look or sound anything like Jesus there was no mistaking the incident. Who else but Jesus could have known it and repeated it in exactly the same way? The incident triggered the recognition. There was no doubt about it. It was Jesus!

Such recognition was always followed by a declaration of faith. "Rabbouni!" "It is the Lord!" It's as if merely recognizing him was not enough. One had to verbalize it, had to say it. The act of faith needs to be externalized. This, too, follows a long standing tradition in the Scriptures where there is power in the uttering of a name. That somehow saying one's name implied making the person present. It's as if they understood that the breath that brought about the creation of Adam when God breathed into his nostrils is the same as the breath we use to utter someone's name. Therefore, it too makes that person come alive; that saying a person's name somehow calls him into being. That's why there were such strong sanctions against uttering the name of God in vain or swearing to a false oath. Recognizing the resurrected Jesus and *uttering his name* or *making an act of faith* are in all the resurrection accounts.

Finally, immediately after the profession of faith Jesus disappears from their sight. After Jesus makes whatever point he wants to make he is gone.

> Then their eyes were opened, and they recognized him; and he vanished from their sight.
> *Luke 24:31*

This is also bothersome. Why didn't Jesus remain and flaunt his resurrection to skeptics and nonbelievers? Once he came back, why didn't he stay around for good? To answer the first question we need to remember that Jesus didn't appear in the expected way. His own followers didn't recognize him so how would others? Even when he appeared in the upper room to the eleven he had to assure Thomas by pointing out the nail imprints in his hands and his wounded side. If people refuse to believe no assurance can ever be enough. They could claim, as others did later, that Jesus didn't really die. That the wine given him on the cross was some kind of drug that made it appear as if he were dead. And so on and on. The answer to the second question requires some honest assessment. Would we really want the dead to come back to life and remain with us? After a while wouldn't we treat them in exactly the same way we always did? Then, what would be the purpose for having them linger on? I'm sure that as much as I loved my mother, if she were to come back again to live with me we would have the same old arguments we always had. Besides, are we really expressing a belief in life after death or are we actually implying a lack of faith in the next life by wanting to hold onto this one for all we're worth? This is tantamount to making this life a form of idolatry.

That seems to be the pattern in all the resurrection accounts. First, no recognition. Then, a trigger point or flash point of recognition. This is followed by a verbalized declaration of faith, usually done by saying the person's name. Finally, the appearance quickly ends.

Since this is what happened in the only resurrection experience in human history, it is logical to assume that other resurrection experiences might follow the same pattern. I believe they do once we know what we're looking for.

· *12* ·

HUDSON STREET

When I was a boy there was next door to my father's grocery store an old abandoned horse barn. It was not a very big barn as it had only two stalls for horses and a small hayloft upstairs. It wasn't used for anything anymore except storing a lot of junk that should have been thrown away. But it was a fun place for us kids and periodically we would play there.

I can recall very vividly one summer afternoon I went up the stairs to the loft to play when I was startled by what I saw on the slanted ceiling in front of me. The entire ceiling was like a giant mural of what was outside. I had been up here countless times before and can assure you that the ceiling was a dingy and dirty gray with absolutely no color, let alone pictures on it. Yet, somehow, the street with cars parked on it and the city housing project across the street were unmistakably pictured there. And in glorious color. As I stared in fascination, I began to notice moving figures in the scene. A car drove by and people walked along the street. I'm sure if there had been television in those days I would have thought that I had stumbled into the "Twilight Zone." It wasn't frightening. It was fascinating if not weird. It was like watching a movie up there in the barn.

I stared in rapt attention. Two ladies encountered each other and began to talk. I could hear what they were saying. This was unbelievable. However, the sound wasn't coming from the picture like at the movie theater. I could hear the voices coming from outside. I walked over to the broken window that faced the street. Below me were the two women. I turned to look at the wall and discovered that the scene had disappeared. I can remember being disappointed and puzzled by what had happened. When I moved away from the window, the scene reappeared. I wondered if there were some kind of magic afoot. I suspect that's what any ten-year-old would think. But I was curious and turned back to the window to watch it disappear once more. That's when the revelation came to me.

In the broken window there was a wedge-shaped piece of glass that was catching the sunlight just right and projecting the image of the outside up against the ceiling. The glass was like a movie projector. The evening sun and the time of year were just right for such a phenomenon to take place. I don't think I could ever duplicate those conditions again no matter how hard I tried. It was like a private screening just for me. It lasted less than half an hour and faded as the sun continued to set. But, the memory has remained with me to this day.

The light projected what was taking place on the street into my private theater. It projected only what was there, not some fantasy as I originally thought. It was the fact that I recognized the ladies and heard them talk that brought me to the truth of what was happening. I was seeing reality, as it was taking place, but in a new way.

God uses the things of this world to teach us about the things of God's world. How could it be otherwise? We can only learn about "there" from what we know about "here." "The kingdom of heaven," Jesus said, "is like a mustard seed." "The resurrection," I say, "is like a ray of light projecting a new reality into the world." Is that what Saint Paul meant when he said that God will give a new form to this lowly body of ours and make it like Jesus' glorified body?

The problem in our generation, and in truth in all generations, is that we look for resurrection to be done according to our will, our expectations. That is why Mary Magdalene in the garden, the disciples on the road to Emmaus, and even the apostles on the Sea of Galilee failed to recognize Jesus when he appeared to them. We are looking for the old form. He is in a new form.

The sunlight on Hudson Street struck the glass and projected what was there in a new way. The ladies were really on the street at that moment even though the reality I saw on the barn ceiling was different. Jesus was really in the garden, on the road, at the seaside even though the reality they all saw was different. That's why they didn't know what to make of it. That's why they were afraid to ask.

Resurrection is a new reality. It was then and still is now. Jesus was alive and recognized but not in the old way, by the old body that died, but by what cannot die, by what can never pass away or be lost—the special, unmistakable ways that he loved people. Mary recognized him in the tender manner in which he called her name. The disciples on the road to Emmaus recognized him in the breaking of the bread. The Apostles on the sea of Galilee knew it was him when they cast their nets at his command and caught a full load of fish. The bodily form may have been new and different but it was undeniably Jesus. "It is the Lord!" they shouted and hurried to him.

From God's perspective there is only one death—Jesus' death on the cross at Calvary. It is as if all deaths from the beginning to the end of time coalesce into one death, one moment. A forever moment. The resurrection, from God's perspective, is at the same moment. That brilliant resurrection moment is projected through all time. When we die we enter that brilliant moment, that broken glass on the cross, and are projected into time and space in a new form. In this glorified body we will be recognized by those who love us and by the special ways in which we loved them.

Resurrection returnings are like private screenings. When Jesus' resurrection light shines through us at our death we will be projected into this world onto the screens of those whose lives we touched with our love. It doesn't have to be a body (ghostly) experience as such. It can happen with a special scent, a certain taste, a song, a touch. What opens the door to these resurrection encounters are the ways that we have touched people's lives. Jesus' resurrection taught us that. The light can only project what's there and only those who know us will recognize us. That's as it must be, for how can we be recognized by those who have never known or experienced us? And when there's no one left who remembers us, the dead will still be alive in Jesus. Then, every time someone shouts, "It's the Lord!" and goes running to him, they will also be running into us.

· 13 ·

GIVE ME SOMETHING
TO REMEMBER YOU BY

When I was a teenager there was a popular song entitled "Oh, Give Me Something to Remember You by." Sentimental songs such as this were very popular in the late forties and fifties, probably because of the war. War has an immediacy about it that brings feelings and values bubbling to the surface. Even though we were too young to have experienced the war we were caught up in the wake of the sentiments that resulted from it. These songs struck a responsive chord in everybody's heart. Of course, we took these words literally and followed the custom of giving to the girl you liked "something to remember you by." Lockets were that kind of gift, the kind that she could put your picture into next to hers and keep them locked in a heart close to her heart. Rings were another such special gift, either graduation or friendship rings. These gifts meant that there was a special bond between the two of you.

The first such gift I gave was my grade-school graduation ring. When I gave it to my very first girlfriend in my freshman year of high school it meant that we were "going steady." A bond was established by our budding adolescent love, which was sealed with a gift given for her to remember me by. Fortunately, I did not sing the song to her or it might have ended the bond even sooner. While the words were sweet and sentimental we were both too young to understand the full import of their meaning. Which is no doubt why she lost the ring shortly thereafter and was not nearly so pained by its loss as I was. We had yet to learn that it was not just simply the giving of a gift no matter how expensive it might be that makes it something to remember you by. It has to have a certain, special quality to make it that. But, we did have one between us, only it was not what either of us planned or expected.

When I first saw her at school I wanted desperately to be around her and talk to her but I didn't even have a way to meet her since we were not in any classes together. Besides, I was painfully shy and could only muster a smile when we passed in the corridor. I would like to have walked her home from school since we both went in the same direction but she always went home with her girlfriend and approaching two of them was even more formidable a task. The opportunity came when I discovered that she was a member of the French club and her girlfriend wasn't. On those days she walked home alone. I decided to wait around after school until the French Club meeting ended and casually "bump" into her. My plans were thwarted however when the janitor kicked me out of the building as I had no legitimate reason to be hanging around after hours. So I waited outside near the door. She came out of a different door. In order to make our encounter look like a chance meeting I had to run around the entire school and approach her from the right direction. I ran like a jackrabbit until I eventually caught up to her.

Trying to appear casual when I was gasping for breath was not an easy thing to do. Nonetheless it worked and we walked together—straight into a cloudburst. The plan called for chivalry only I didn't have an umbrella and she was already wearing a jacket. So I gave her my baseball cap. "It'll at least keep your head dry," I said. When I dropped her off at home, she kept the cap. That became the gift for her to remember me by—more than the ring. She talked about the cap all during the year we went together and kept it even after we broke up. When she learned all I had gone through to meet her it was the cap that took on special meaning and not my class ring.

It is also that way throughout our lives. Countless couples tell me about simple things they gave each other when they were first married and poor as church mice that have more meaning in their lives than the many more and costlier things they have since given one another. One man keeps in his medicine cabinet, in spite of innumerable moves, the shaving mug and brush his wife gave him when they first got married even though he now shaves only electrically. "I would sooner leave my right hand behind," he told me when I discovered the relic in his bathroom cabinet. These are those special gifts we give one another that reach deep into our hearts and are forever memorable. That's what the song means when it asks for something to remember you by.

On the road to Emmaus the disciples rediscovered that that was precisely what Jesus had given them. In spite of the fact that he walked along with them they were restrained from recognizing him at first. What would trigger the recognition? The account tells us that while he spoke to them their hearts were on fire. But, even that was not enough. Others could set one's heart on fire. It was unquestionably the breaking of the bread. This was the gift that Jesus had once given them that became something to remember Him by. They had no doubt been present on another occasion or occasions when Jesus had touched them deeply by performing this act. One can almost assume from the context that it must have been the multiplication of the loaves in the desert. If they had never seen Jesus do this very thing before and been moved by it, how could they have recognized him by it? That gift became the door that opened for Jesus and them an afterdeath, a resurrection experience. The gift was the trigger that opened the door to remembrance and resurrection. It is what the Church for earliest times called a sacrament, a sacred gift. A sacrament is that special gift Jesus gave as an expression of his love, a gift that we are meant to remember him by. If we want a resurrection experience with him we bring out the gift, we remember, and we believe. The sacrament becomes the door for a real resurrection experience with Jesus. We don't look for the old body in the old way but the new presence in a new way.

We also can do what Jesus did. Because of our love we can give to others gifts that they will remember us by. These are the sacraments that exist between us. These also become doorways for afterdeath experiences with those we love. Just as Jesus comes back to those who love him through his sacraments with us, those who died come back to us through the gifts they gave us to remember them by.

· 14 ·

A TIME FOR
REMEMBERING

*D*eath is a time of remembrance. It is a time to remember all the special, wonderful, and happy times we shared with the deceased. We recall all the unique events that touched our lives—graduations, weddings, births, anniversaries; the wonderful places where we celebrated life together—the schools we attended, the trips and vacations we took, the private and intimate places so meaningful and personal to us; and of course, the happy times that become the sugar in the dark coffee of our old age. That's what wakes are for. That's what funerals are all about.

Why do we reminisce about the dead? Because memories are our way of holding on to the deceased for a little while longer. As long as we talk about them we keep them from slipping into oblivion where they would be lost in the abyss forever. Before Jesus we could only hope to keep their memory alive to the second or third generation. Great grandchildren have little or no recollection of their great grandparents.

While the hope was for the just to be held in everlasting remembrance, the possibility was indeed remote unless you were of the stature of a Moses or David.

Before Jesus stories were simply vehicles for remembering. They died when there was no one left to remember and tell them. After Jesus they became doorways to resurrection. Is this not what the Gospel accounts of Jesus' resurrection are trying to tell us? Mary Magdalene had her story—the special way in which Jesus called her by name. This story opened the door for her recognizing the resurrected Jesus at the tomb. The old story with its profound and soul-stirring implications doesn't die. Quite the contrary—a new story is born from it. It lives with a new life. A new dimension has been added to it. The same holds true for the other resurrection experiences of Jesus. Old stories become the link to new realities. Jesus is not simply remembered for his memorable distribution of the loaves and fish in the desert or at seder meals, days or years ago, but because of his breaking bread with the disciples in the inn that day— three days after his death!

Stories which heretofore were merely reminiscences are now open doors for the deceased to come back to us in resurrection. When we speak of them, we recall them from the place of death into the present and they become alive once more. They resurrect, no matter how briefly. However, once the connection is made and the reality is perceived, it is enough. It truly is enough. We are all deeply desirous of keeping our loved ones with us for as long as possible while they are alive. However, it would be an entirely different matter if they were to return from the grave to be with us. A brief encounter is more than sufficient. I doubt many of us would be able to handle any more than that no matter how much the deceased were loved. We need only the assurance that they are still alive, even if in some new dimension. Therein also lies our fervent hope for eventual reunion.

In the meantime we are called to share our love with anyone and everyone we meet along the way, just as Jesus taught. This is how we open more and more doors for our own resurrection, for our own return into the lives of those we love, no matter how briefly. The more special times, places, and experiences (touch points, sacraments) we share, the more opportunities we will have to be recalled by our loved ones. To come back more often afterwards, we have to love more now.

· 15 ·

EMIL

*E*mil was a big man. Six feet tall and "somewhat more than 250 pounds" (a bit somewhat more), he had what the French would call *joie de vivre*, a zest for life. He would aptly be described by countless people as the most unforgettable character they ever met. For a man who held no public office, no rank in civic organizations, and a modest status job as a real-estate broker, his circle of friends literally extended to hundreds of people. (At least six hundred people attended his funeral on Christmas Eve.)

He was a presence wherever he went, but never an ostentatious one. He was hardly ever the center of attention; nor did he crave it. He simply had a remarkable way of making everyone in the room with him feel special, even the proverbial wallflower with whom he always spent extra time. He was so full of life it was contagious, even bothersome at times. At a family cottage on the lake, he would never let the sun go down without an audience. No matter what people were doing at the time—usually sitting down for dinner or playing cards—he would roust everyone, forcibly if necessary, and herd us outside to watch the sun sink majestically into the lake. In spite of our protests, we would all take a moment to stare at it in silent and rapt attention. When it was over Emil would give us permission to go back and continue whatever we were doing.

No party was ever a flop if Emil was there, although to his wife's dismay, they hosted almost all of them. He invariably concocted some bizarre culinary delicacies which left everyone licking their chops. And if, there should be a lull in the activities, he would be certain to urge the group into a lively sing-along.

When he died of a heart attack just before Christmas he left a gaping hole in many lives. We all knew that someone very special was irretrievably lost to us. Or was he? Early, the following summer a group of us were gathered at the family cottage once again. We were all busily involved in whatever we were doing when someone looked out the window and said, "Look everybody. It's an Emil sunset." Without even being summoned we all dropped what we were doing and went outside to watch the blazing sun go down. No one spoke. At that moment, we all knew that Emil was actually there with us. He was present to us because he had left us the sunset as his sacrament and we all knew it and felt it.

Years later on another occasion, one of our friends was celebrating a sixtieth birthday party. It was a nice celebration but rather subdued because there were cliques of people sticking together because they didn't know each other. It was a situation that desperately called for Emil. I had no sooner mentioned it than the disc jockey played an obscure fifties' song that just happened to be one of Emil's favorites. Those of us who knew Emil hurried over to the young disc jockey to ask him where he got ahold of that record. He said that when he first heard it, he thought it rather unique and went out of his way to get a copy of it. At that particular moment he felt the urge to dig it up from his collection and play it. At that moment, Emil was telling us that he had come to the party.

Somewhere it was said, "To those who believe no explanation is necessary and to those who don't believe no explanation is possible." There's no way of proving that Emil was present on these and other occasions. To those of us who knew and loved him, we believe beyond a doubt that he was there with us.

Such occurrences have happened to untold numbers of people. They are usually dismissed as hysteria, emotion, or madness. Consequently, people have a tendency not to talk about them when they happen in their lives. They will tell you, as I have been told many times, that they are afraid to tell others of these experiences because people will think they're crazy. So they keep them to themselves. This is truly unfortunate because one of the steps in resurrection experiences is an expressed and verbalized profession of faith. Breath gives the experience life just as it does us. To hold one's breath is to close the door to future resurrection experiences and to future returnings.

· 16 ·

RETURNINGS

When Ann F.'s husband died she felt that there was still something unresolved in his passing that would not let her accept his death peacefully. Even though he was a good man, he wasn't much of a churchgoer and she feared that he might not have made it to paradise. This worry kept her distracted during the day and wakeful at night. Finally, one night she dreamt that he was sitting in his familiar easy chair with a contented look on his face. She was quite explicit in relating to me that although he never spoke a word to her she knew that he was assuring her that he was all right. She woke up immediately afterwards with a sense of well-being and relief.

Taking it to be no more than a wish-fulfillment dream, she let it go at that. A few days later she received a phone call from her married son who told her that he had dreamt that very same night that his father, seated in the same familiar chair, assured him that he was all right even though he never spoke a word to him. The same dream, the same night communicating the same message in the same unique way to two different people. Some would take it as no more than coincidence. To Ann it was a resurrection experience.

When "Da Da" died in rural England, his grandson told me, his wife decided that she was too old to take care of his pet pigeons so she sold them off and got rid of the coops. Several years later she was taken to an old folks' home to live out her days. When it became evident that she would not last much longer she asked her children to let her return home to die. They agreed and hired a nurse to take care of her. Late one afternoon a large flock of pigeons came and settled on the place where the coops used to be. "Da Da has come for me," she told the nurse who had no idea what she was talking about. Later when the nurse passed her room she noticed an old gentleman seated at her bedside. Curious as to who it might be she quickly returned to find the man gone and the old woman dead. "The pigeons had not been there for years prior to or since," the grandson assured me.

A family friend tells the story of a favorite maiden aunt who had the "unladylike" habit of whistling wherever she went. In spite of her family's protests she never stopped, much to the delight of her nieces who not only encouraged her but imitated her. At least twenty years after she died, my friend, married and with children of her own, tells the story of how she was standing in line at a supermarket checkout when a woman ahead of her suddenly started whistling. As she describes it:

> From behind, she looked exactly like my aunt. It so startled me that I got the goose bumps. I just had to go up to her and look her in the face. I tapped her on the shoulder and when she turned around I was totally embarrassed as she looked nothing like my aunt.

She further explained, "Until she turned around I would have sworn that it was my aunt." The point is she was having a resurrection experience without realizing it. Her aunt had left her with that special sacrament, the whistling, which had opened for them the door to a resurrection return. For a moment her aunt was alive again and whistling for her. She acknowledged it and the return ended.

A further point should not be overlooked. Her expectation, whether conscious or subconscious, was to find her aunt *as she was* in her body form. She was looking in the wrong place. As a matter of fact the body became a deterrent to the experience. It ended the moment she realized that the woman didn't look like her aunt. She might have enjoyed it a while longer had she not been driven to "prove" what was happening.

Resurrection appearances are not always confined to body experiences. My findings indicate that there seem to be far more nonbody returnings. Animals are often a link with the deceased.

C. M. lost her twelve-year-old son Robbie in an automobile accident just before Christmas. Not long after the funeral, she, her husband, daughter and remaining ten-year-old son went to the family cottage at the shore hoping to find some healing. Whenever the family went there during vacation times Robbie loved to wander along the beach and play with the seagulls. When they returned to the shore, the following incident, told in C. M.'s own words, occurred:

> My husband and son were silently tossing a football back and forth as I walked along the shore. No one spoke. A small cluster of seagulls appeared a few feet away at the edge of the water. One white bird with black-tipped wings turned to look at my husband and son. He left the other birds and began to walk over to them, slowly and deliberately, stopping when he stood precisely between them. They continued aimlessly tossing the football, not really looking at anything. They didn't see the bird. I watched as the gull looked from one to the other, back and forth following the flight of the ball over and over. I felt that the bird wanted to play. My skin

started to feel prickly. The bird seemed to want them to see him and waited patiently until they did. Suddenly, my son noticed him and tossed the ball to him. The bird effortlessly lifted off the sand, without hurry, easily avoiding the ball. He circled slowly a foot or two above each of their heads in graceful arcs. He then glided over to the peak of a tile roof I could see just peeking above the nearest sand dune. The *instant* he landed and turned toward the sea, a narrow shaft of pure sunlight cut through the clouds and engulfed him. Everything else was heavy with gray cold, but the bird stood steadily gazing up into a beam of full sunlight. He stood motionless for about a minute until the sun faded behind the clouds. Then he flew slowly away, heading inland.

I was crying by then. My heart and mind were both telling me that our Robbie had been in that bird, reassuring us that he was vividly alive and intensely joyous. I felt he was saying that he loved us, *that he would come as close as he could and to look for him.* (Italics mine)

C. M.

Had this mother been fixated on notions of bodily (ghostly) resurrection as so many are, she might have missed her son's return in a new and sacramental presence. Robbie would then be confined only to a physical look-alike like my friend's aunt. He had left behind many sacramental signs that would open the door for him to be present at other times and in other ways. From the same letter:

> Many times over the years I've had the feeling he has been in some playful animal, in autumn leaves springing up to dance just for me, in the precise pitch of his voice in a boy I'll see running on a soccer field. "Hi Mom! I'm here. Don't worry . . . it's awesome!"

J. G., a woman from Missouri, related how after the recent loss of her husband, an outdoorsman and a hunter, she went for a ride in the country with her son. As they drove along recalling the memories still fresh in their minds her son noticed that they were driving through an area where he and his dad had hunted in the past. She asked him to stop so they could get out and walk. As they did her son either picked or took out (I can't recall) a persimmon commenting on how much his father loved them. At that moment, a deer came out of the woods and approached them. She was so startled by this unexpected turn of events that she couldn't move. The deer stood an arm's length away just looking at them. Her son then held out the persimmon to the deer, who took it and ran off. The experience was so overwhelming that they were visibly shaken for a while. She ended her account by saying, "I know it was him. How many deer in the wild have you heard about that would come up and take something out of your hand?"

"None, that I know of," I said.

There are innumerable doorways to resurrection returnings. They come in all shapes, at unexpected times, and in the most unlikely ways. It seems that all that is needed is openness.

During the Christmas season I submitted my dad's name for "A Tree for Life," a project put on by Hospice. Names of the deceased were written on a card, tied with a red ribbon and hung on an outside Christmas tree. There was a tree-lighting ceremony, which I attended with a neighbor.

It was very beautiful, but it just didn't feel right to me. There were hundreds of names on this tree and I couldn't find my dad's. I looked and looked, the whole time thinking what am I doing here? This is all very nice but it's not the kind of thing my dad would do. Why am I bothering? It's freezing out here and I can't find his name.

My neighbor suggested we go inside the building and look around. I grudgingly said OK when all I wanted to do was go home and feel sorry for myself. I walked in this building and the first thing I saw were gorgeous plaster ceilings—very intricate work and just stunning. My father was a *plasterer!* It was just the kind of work he did. It was as if *he* had written his name *there* for *me.* (Italics mine)

R. S.

Time and again people have spoken about "returnings" associated with music. Music has always had the ability to draw people into personal intimacy with it and one another and at the same time give that relationship a kind of eternal quality. This is "our song."

My husband died suddenly about eight years ago. Our youngest daughter was about to enter her sophomore year in college at the time. She had always been extremely close to him . . . so his loss was very difficult for her.

The night before her graduation we went out to dinner to celebrate the great occasion. Since the restaurant was filled with many other parents, they took our names and sent us promptly to the lounge for a drink or two. My daughter and I ordered our "favorites" and were about to toast each other when the guitarist started to play "Mr. Bojangles," which had been one of my husband's favorite songs that he, too, would play on his guitar. We looked at each other with tears in our eyes. I also felt a shiver go up my spine. I said to her, "He's here with us," and she said, "I know." The very next song he played was also a favorite of D's (husband), "You picked a fine time to leave me Lucille." This experience was not just a memory. My daughter and I felt that he was there with us.

M. J.

Another letter relates music as an answer to prayer.

My brother at age sixty-one died of a massive heart attack. I was heartbroken as I never had any sisters and only the one brother. I prayed for him day and night to the extent that I wasn't getting enough sleep. I asked God to send me a sign that he was in heaven so I could have peace of mind. One morning at about 5:30 a.m. one of my music boxes started to play for about twenty seconds. I hadn't played any of them for over a year. I just knew in my heart that God had given me my sign and now I am at peace when I think of my brother.

M. H.

There is even room for the bizarre in resurrection occurrences. One mother told me how her son's friend who would stay on overnights at their house was the only one who knew how to get the third-floor shower working. It was no simple task, she informed me, because it took pliers and a screwdriver to do it each time. The youth died tragically and during one of the nights of his wake, in the middle of the night the shower went on by itself.

In yet another such "middle of the night" event a family told me how during one of the nights of their mother's wake the vacuum cleaner suddenly turned on.

Children are often the recipients of resurrection experiences. Here, too, there are innumerable stories of children talking to the dead. We dismiss them as childhood fantasies and fabrications because of our deep-rooted adult prejudices. Occasionally, however, something occurs along with these appearances that jars our incredulity.

There is the story of Claire H. of Ireland who three days after the death and burial of her mother came out of the shower and as she hurriedly passed the living room she noticed that her two sons Daniel (five years) and David (two years) were talking to someone. In her bedroom she wondered who might be visiting her cottage so she threw on a wrap and went into the living room. No one was there.

"Who were you boys talking to a moment ago?" she asked.

"Nana," they both replied.

Even after assuring them that it couldn't have been

their grandmother, the boys stuck to their story and even related what they had talked about. She was so troubled by their obstinacy that she decided to take them to their aunt's next door for "a good talking to." As they passed the outside window of the living room the boys pointed and she saw her mother standing there.

A sunset, a baseball cap, a school ring, seagulls, deer, a whistle, a house, a chair, a tee shirt, a favorite flower, a song, a familiar perfume—these can all be things we remember each other by. These can also be sacraments that we establish with one another.

There are innumerable people with countless such stories. Once you are open to hearing them, most of them will freely tell you all about them. The very telling not only keeps more than just the memories of our loved ones alive, but allows the door to remain open for further resurrection experiences. However, if there is no openness, no faith, there is no way to reach beyond the narrow world of the unquestionably provable. There will also never be a resurrection returning.

· *17* ·

CONSIDER THE RAINBOW

When my best friend's mother died, it was like losing my own mother once again. It was almost just as painful both times. I stopped and wondered if I had the power that Jesus had and could say to her, "Good woman—arise!" would I do it? In all honesty I probably would because no less than others I would like to hold on to those who were beloved and special in my life. But, the thought also brought some serious reflection.

If I could bring her back it should not be without the prospect of some major physical changes. First of all, her heart was weak, which was what gave out on her and caused her death. She would have to be given a new heart almost immediately or she would quickly die again. Since we have the technology to give someone another heart, that might not be a major obstacle. However, she also had poor eyes which caused her no end of pain and frustration. I suppose we could give her whatever corrective surgery she might need, even a corneal transplant if necessary. After giving her someone else's heart and eyes, we might also find it necessary to give her a new kidney. She also had bad hearing. I could go on and add a hip and knee replacement both of which would be extremely beneficial to her restoration. I suppose if we had to, we could give her replacement parts for just about every part of her body—heart, lungs, liver, kidneys, pituitary.

What if, however, each body part that was replaced would have the effect of changing who she was to some degree. A replacement heart would change part of her personality because of it. A new kidney would change her some more. A new liver, pituitary, lung and so on would all have a cumulative effect on her ego. At some point we might want to stop altogether, at least before we get to the point of no return and it would no longer be her. Otherwise, why bother restoring her life?

But, as we already know, that doesn't happen. Past experience has proven this not to be the case. No matter how many replacement parts we give people, their personalities remain unaltered, they all continue to be the same person afterward as before. What this is saying then is that we are more than just our bodies. As beautiful or as plain as we may be, as strong or as weak, as healthy or as sick—who we are goes beyond the merely physical. We are more than the sum total of our body parts.

Supposing we were to take water and pour it out on the ground. In the splash tiny droplets, some microscopic, would rise up like mist from a waterfall. In the blazing sunlight a single drop could become transfixed as the purifying sun shone through it. When the light gets "prismed" through it a new form emerges—a rainbow.

Saint Paul says that this lowly body of ours will take on a new form and become like Jesus' glorified body. The Jesus who was transfigured on the mountain, who became as dazzling light before the Apostles, becomes the sun that shines through space and time. When his light transfixes the single drop of water that was my friend's mother when her life was poured out, she took on a new form. She has become glorious as the sun (Son). She is now a part of the resurrection rainbow.

God said to Noah, "I will put a bow in the sky as a reminder to you" of my covenant, of my love. There will be no more death the old way. This shall be a sign of life.

If we try to hold onto the body, the way it was, as precious as it was, we are holding it back from all that it can become. That's why Jesus told his beloved Mary Magdalene, "Do not touch me." Or in the original Aramaic, "Do not hold on to me." I want to be set free. Besides, you can't grab hold of a rainbow.

When a drop of water rises and is purified by the sun, it leaves behind what cannot be raised. The minerals, the residues get left behind. There is a momentary purifying flash when we see the rainbow. Then, only the pure form continues on to ascend to the sun. So shall it be with those who die in Christ. What cannot

be raised, the old body, is left behind. The dead are
set free.

> So it is with the resurrection of the dead.
> What is sown is perishable, what is raised
> is imperishable. It is sown in dishonor, it is
> raised in glory. It is sown in weakness, it is
> raised in power. It is sown a physical body, it
> is raised a spiritual body. If there is a physical
> body, there is also a spiritual body.
>
> *1 Corinthians 15:42–44*

What I am saying, brothers and sisters, is
this: flesh and blood cannot inherit the kingdom of God, nor does the perishable inherit
the imperishable. Listen, I will tell you a
mystery! We will not all die, but we will all
be changed, in a moment, in the twinkling of
an eye, at the last trumpet. For the trumpet
will sound, and the dead will be raised imperishable, and we will be changed. For this perishable body must put on imperishability,
and this mortal body must put on immortality. When this perishable body puts on imperishability, and this mortal body puts on
immortality, then the saying that is written
will be fulfilled: "Death has been swallowed

up in victory. Where, O death, is your victory? Where, O death, is your sting?"

1 Corinthians 15:50–55

If we wish to see the dead once again we need only look to Jesus or at the rainbow.

LET'S BE PRACTICAL

*P*erhaps we should also consider a very practical point about resurrection—absolute certitude. Resurrection is now and always will be a matter of faith. It must always be so because there is absolutely no way that the physical can prove the spiritual. They are two completely different and separate realities. We may have what is called the certitude of faith, but we can never have the certitude of science.

> Faith is the assurance of things hoped for, the conviction of things not seen.
>
> *Hebrews 11:1*

In the case of resurrection this may not be such a bad thing. Supposing the afterlife were the way people constantly imagine it to be, that is, our resurrected bodies becoming ghosts that we could see and talk to. Supposing my deceased mother were to reappear to me in a way that was unmistakable, that I could question and determine with absolute certitude that it was her, whether my hand could pass through her or not. What would be the first question I or any of us would ask? What's it like? What is life after death like?

There are only three possible answers to that question—good, bad, or indifferent. Consider what would happen if we were to know beyond any shadow of a doubt that it is good. This knowledge would no longer come from Scripture or tradition or faith but because I am discovering it face-to-face (scientific certitude). How would that affect my life? Or all our lives if we were all to experience the same thing? (We would each have to experience it ourselves, because taking someone else's word for it would be faith.)

For many of us, if things got pretty rough—physically, mentally, or emotionally—we would most likely just opt out. We'd say, "Why bother? Let's just end this life and hurry to the next one." Why should we wait? Why would we want to wait? If I get sick or in difficult financial straits, why would I bother to suffer? Let me get it over with now and get to the next place where it's better forever.

Let's be perfectly frank. There would even be people who if they got a bad headache would say, "To hell with this. I'm going to heaven." If life this side of heaven is a struggle, and it most assuredly is, why on earth would we bother putting up with it? Who among us wouldn't take the easiest way out if it were open to us? Who among us if we were living difficult or marginal lives in New York City and were unconditionally promised a full, secure, worry-free life in New Jersey would hesitate to cross the Hudson River? Ask the myriad immigrants who left families and homelands to come to America for a mere glimmer of hope for a better life.

Then, think of what this would do to society. What society? Who would want to bother? What kind of a world would result? What kind of planning, building, working could there possibly be in such an environment?

You see, it may be precisely that tiny, little shadow of a doubt upon which this world is built. It is very likely that tiny, little shadow of a doubt that moves us to take this earth and subdue it, take this creation and improve it, give names to the animals, till the soil and increase and multiply. If for no other reason than that one in the hand is worth two in the bush.

That is a very real possibility if it were provable that there is an afterlife and that it is good. An afterlife that is bad or indifferent I will leave to your own imagination.

If we admit to a shadow of a doubt, no matter how small, does that mean we lack faith? I suppose it all depends upon one's concept of faith. If you consider faith as all or nothing, then it is a lack of faith. If you are like the Apostle Peter who shouted, "Lord, I believe. Help my unbelief," then you admit to degrees of faith. It is in this tension that we work creatively.

So if my mother were able to show up in a way that was unmistakable—considering the consequences, I'd prefer she didn't. In the long run faith tells us that God knows what he's doing. I'd personally have no faith in our trying to run the show.

· 19 ·

EASTER

The women were terrified and bowed their
faces to the ground, but the men said to
them, "Why do you look for the living
among the dead? He is not here, but has
risen."

Luke 24:5

You will search for me, but you will not find
me; and where I am, you cannot come.

John 7:34

For where two or three are gathered in my
name, I am there among them.

Matthew 18:20

Although these three Scripture passages do not follow sequentially in the Gospels, they could very
well when speaking of resurrection realities. Jesus is
gone. In this body we cannot follow. He returns in a
new way. The same can and will be said of us one day.

When trying to explain the wonder of the resurrection to children one Easter I carried a big balloon into
their midst.

"Who would like to play with this wonderful balloon?" I asked.

As expected, every hand flew up.

"Well, I've only one balloon," I said. "So, I'll just have to let Chrissy play with it."

To her delight and the others' dismay I put the balloon in Chrissy's outstretched hands. She eagerly took it and began playing with it, tossing it into the air and catching it while the others watched hungrily. After a few moments I asked her if she would be willing to share the balloon with Joey seated at the other end of the room. She had to be coaxed but she agreed and I brought the balloon over to him. Again, I waited for a while and then asked Joey if he would be willing to share it with someone else in another part of the room. After a few more times, I showed exasperation and commented, "There's too many of you and only one balloon. Besides, it's taking up too much time to go from one person to another and let each one have a turn. Wouldn't it be wonderful if I could get this same balloon to everyone at the same time?"

They all tried to gather around it but there were too many of them for it to work. Their frustration became apparent.

"Well, Jesus was in the same predicament. Everybody wanted him. His friends wanted him in Nazareth. His cousins wanted him in Bethany. The Galileans wanted him to work miracles in Galilee and the Judeans wanted him to teach them in Jerusalem.

And they all wanted him at the same time. Besides, we want Jesus with us here today, too. What could he do?"

Truly, what could he do? He had to get out of the body which was confining him to one place at one time. He had to be set free to be in all places at all times at the same time. There's just no way that the physical body can do this. But not the spiritual body. It can.

So I took a needle and burst the balloon. "Now the air, the spirit that filled the balloon, the body of Jesus has been set free. Now Jesus can be anywhere and in anything or anyone he wants. It's the same Jesus," I assured them, "only different."

Saint Paul writes about how we are all one body but many parts.[1] So it is with Christ. We are all his members. Jesus is in all of us. In another letter he reminds Christians that in Jesus there is no more Greek or Jew, male or female, slave or free.[2] If Jesus were to return as a ghost would we ever see him in a woman, a neighbor, or perhaps even an enemy? I believe that it is better that we don't know or should ever know what he looked like. We would doubtless go around saying that Tom, Dick, and Harry don't look anything like him. To say nothing of Mary. He has entered the ages. He is timeless. We need to get away from the idolatry of the body, the obsession with the physical, the tyranny of the here and now.

With the resurrection we are set free from our suffocating stereotypes. We can see him where two or three are gathered in his name without trying to pick out which one or ones specifically. We can see him in the breaking of bread, even though a loaf of bread in no way resembles Jesus. We can see him at weddings and funerals because he touched us at Cana and at the tomb of Lazarus leaving us a sacrament, something to remember him by. We can see him in Chicago, Rome, and Sydney at the same time. This is his glory and our hope. Because if it happened to him who was the first fruits,[3] the forerunner, it will happen to us. For we believe that where the master is, there the disciples will be.

My mother died when I was just twenty-one years old. As a young woman, newly married and just beginning my adult life, I was, and probably will always be, quite devastated by her death. Over the years (twenty-nine to be exact) she has always made herself very apparent in my life but it's only been the last nine or ten that I've really come to know and recognize when she's present. I always called on her when I needed help and nothing else seemed to work. She has been my constant connection to God. Through this awareness I have grown and I now realize that she has been more help to me dead than alive. I never, ever thought I could say such a thing. I just know that with having such a close connection to God, she has always been there for me whenever I needed her. If she were still on earth I would be sharing her with my six brothers and sisters, not to mention all the other people who knew and loved her as much as I did. I know she's present to all our family but now she can be there for all of us all of the time.

K. M.

NOTES

1. 1 Corinthians 13:12ff.
2. "There is no longer Jew or Greek, there is no longer slave or free, there is no longer male and female; for all of you are one in Christ Jesus" (Galatians 3:28).
3. 1 Corinthians 15:20.

EPILOGUE

He [Jesus] answered them, "When it is evening, you say, 'It will be fair weather, for the sky is red.' And in the morning, 'It will be stormy today, for the sky is red and threatening.' You know how to interpret the appearance of the sky. How is it that you cannot interpret the signs of the times?"

Matthew 16:2–3